Written by
Christopher Maynard

Edited by
Graham Marks

Designed by
Jonathan Lambert

Illustrated by
Gary Andrews
John Bolton
Alan Case
Phil Davis
John Farman
Alicia Garcia de Lynam
Oscar Grillo
Lin Jammet
Ainslie Mc. Leod
David Simonds
Roger Wade Walker

© **Guinness Superlatives Ltd. 1986**

Published in Great Britain by Guinness Superlatives Ltd.,
33 London Road, Enfield, Middlesex EN2 6DJ

**Produced for the Publishers by
Keith Faulkner Publishing Ltd.**

**'Guinness' is a registered trade mark of Guinness
Superlatives Ltd.**

British Library Cataloguing in Publication Data

[Guinness book of records. *Selections*]
Apple peelers and coin stackers: and other amazing
human records from the Guinness book of records.
1. Curiosities and wonders—Juvenile literature
I. [Guinness book of records. *Selections]*
032'.02   AG243

ISBN 0-85112-471-2

Typeset by Kalligraphics Ltd. Printed and bound in
Italy by New Interlitho SPA Milan

APPLE PEELERS AND COIN STACKERS...

GUINNESS BOOKS

WHAT GOES UP...

In America they pitch baseballs. In Norway they pitch forks. Contests have been held here since 1914, and when Trond Ulleberg, farmboy favourite, set the pitchfork record in 1978, he reached a height of 19.8m (65ft). Unlike baseball, there was no catcher.

In America, where rolling pins are used on the heads of husbands much as on pies, a toss of 53m (175ft) by Lori La Deane Adams won her the record. The man in her life applauded – from a safe distance!

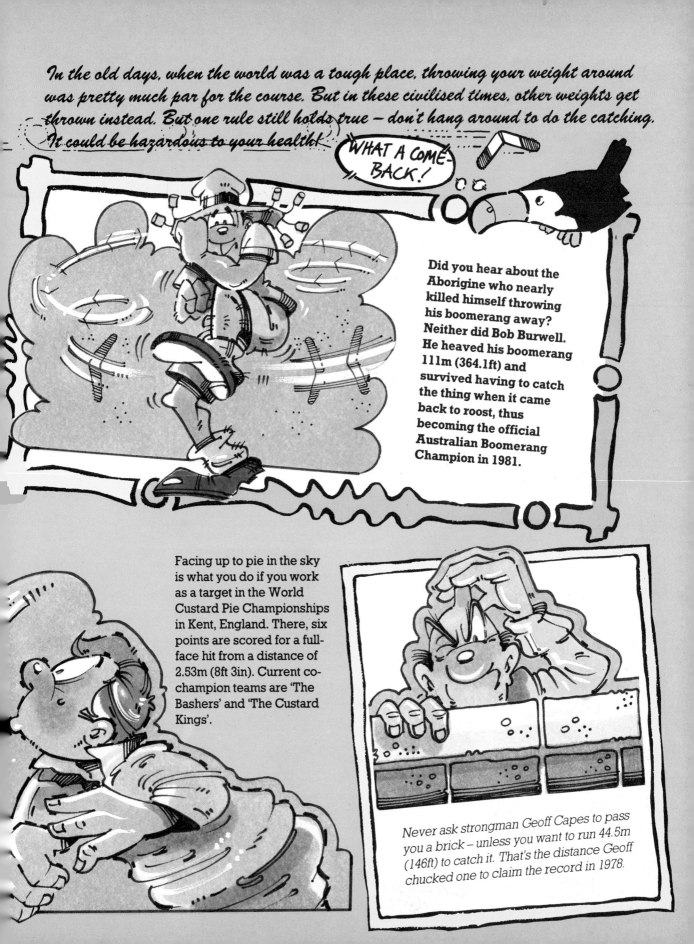

In the old days, when the world was a tough place, throwing your weight around was pretty much par for the course. But in these civilised times, other weights get thrown instead. But one rule still holds true – don't hang around to do the catching. It could be hazardous to your health!

WHAT A COME-BACK!

Did you hear about the Aborigine who nearly killed himself throwing his boomerang away? Neither did Bob Burwell. He heaved his boomerang 111m (364.1ft) and survived having to catch the thing when it came back to roost, thus becoming the official Australian Boomerang Champion in 1981.

Facing up to pie in the sky is what you do if you work as a target in the World Custard Pie Championships in Kent, England. There, six points are scored for a full-face hit from a distance of 2.53m (8ft 3in). Current co-champion teams are 'The Bashers' and 'The Custard Kings'.

Never ask strongman Geoff Capes to pass you a brick – unless you want to run 44.5m (146ft) to catch it. That's the distance Geoff chucked one to claim the record in 1978.

DON'T SNEEZE!

When is a high-wire act a crime? When it's on a wire stretched 110 storeys up – 441m (1350ft) high – between the twin towers of the World Trade Center. That's what Phillipe Petit discovered when nabbed for criminal trespass.

A..A..A... ..CHOO!!

Build a tower of coins, 205 high, and you would win just about any bar contest in the world. When they are balanced on a coin standing vertically with another as its base, then you've just been beaten by Bruce McConachy of Vancouver, BC.

Nobody dared sneeze when John Sain built a house of cards. His ultimate construction was more a skyscraper than a house. He erected 68 storeys. Topping out ceremonies took place a 3.73m (12ft 3in).

There are times when a steady hand and strong nerves are not quite enough — when you're someone who's reputation is in the balance. If you want to stack up the records, you need the ability to ignore life's little distractions — like the fly that always lands on your nose when you're one step from success!

Flamingoes do it. Ballet dancers do it. But not the way V. S. Kumar Anandan does it. He knocked spots off them all by spending 33hr balancing on one foot!

Perhaps 7 is a lucky number in Charlotte, North Caroline. How else do you explain the way Lang Martin balanced seven golf balls, one on top of another.

Doorstep service is one thing, but in Jamaica, New York they deliver milk the hard way. Ashrita (look Ma, no hands!) Furman walked 38.6km (24 miles) balancing a full pint on his head without once losing his bottle.

COLLECTOMANIA!

Not counting duty free shops at airports, the world's biggest selection of different cigarette brands is that of Dr Robert Kaufman of New York City. His collection of 7855 packs, from 172 countries, is so large it makes him puff just to count them.

After 34 years of dedicated work, Helge Friholm's world-beating collection of bottle caps came to 34,306 different kinds. That's two new caps per day, every day of the year, with no breaks for week-ends or holidays!

ANIMALS SHOULD KNOW BETTER!

When Edward Giaccone throws a party it's either whisky galore or one giant headache. Or both. His is the world's largest collection of whisky bottles, with some 3100 different brands behind the bar.

Squirrels store, rats hoard, but people collect. In each case the instinct is the same. The difference is that people also insist on showing off their collections to their fellow man – usually with a lot of fuss and excitement. The grandest and showiest collections of all are known as museums.

Walter Cavanagh – The Owe Boy – has 1173 valid credit cards. He uses a 76.2m (250ft) wallet and reckons his credit to be worth $1.25 million. Now if he could just find a restaurant that accepts them all . . .

NON!

YOU'VE GOT TO GIVE HIM CREDIT!

!?

When it comes to being single-minded, the prize should go to The Labologists Society of Britain. Their collection of 27,845 labels comes from one product only. You guessed it; they're only here for beer!

When Arthur Jordan of Virginia, USA wanted to show the folks his 710,000 can tops, he laid them out in a straight line. Friends found that a stroll to see Arthur's collection was more like a hike – of 18.02km (11.2 miles) to be exact.

JUMP TO IT...

Guy Stewart, the man with more bounce than a kangaroo, spent the 8–9th March 1985, jumping up and down in one spot. In the process he set a pogo stick jumping record of 130,077 consecutive leaps.

If you'll believe that the long metal flaps over the top of motorcycle wheels are wings then you'll believe anything. Perhaps that's what helped Alain Prieur of France to leap his motorcycle 64.6m (212ft) over a line of 16 buses. Talk about jumping a bus queue!

Eighteen barrels, laid on the ice, are not something to skate over lightly. That's what Yvon Jolin of Canada discovered. Instead, he skate-hopped them with a single flying leap of 8.99m (29ft 5in).

LOOKS LIKE A BARREL OF LARFS!

There's something about flying through the air that appeals to the birdbrain in all of us. Maybe it's our lack of wings, or the fact that we're heavier than air. Whatever the cause, at the end of the day people will go to incredible lengths to find ways of staying airbourne.

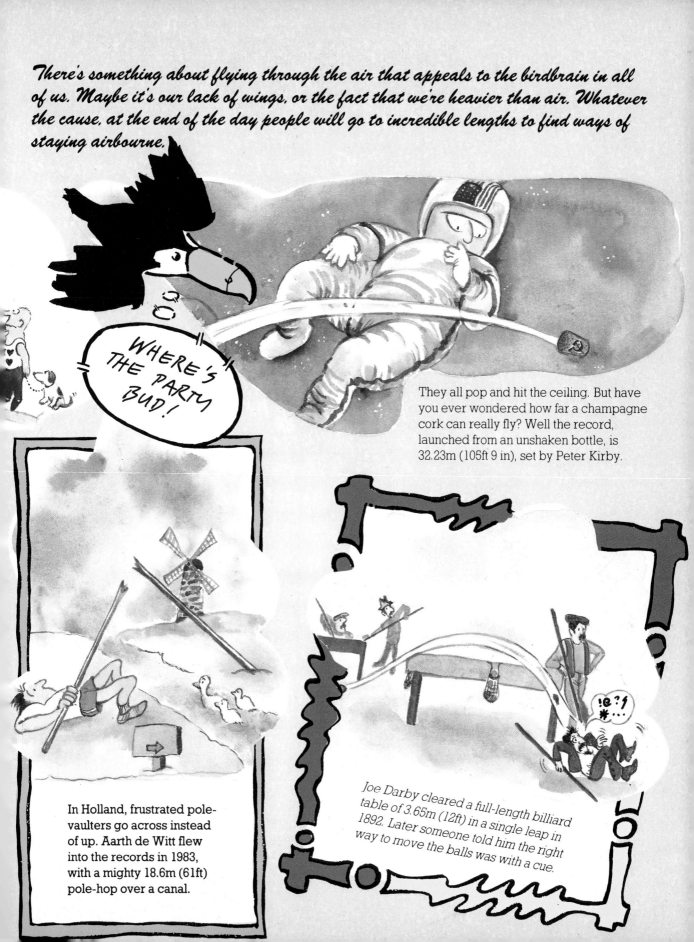

WHERE'S THE PARTY BUD!

They all pop and hit the ceiling. But have you ever wondered how far a champagne cork can really fly? Well the record, launched from an unshaken bottle, is 32.23m (105ft 9 in), set by Peter Kirby.

In Holland, frustrated pole-vaulters go across instead of up. Aarth de Witt flew into the records in 1983, with a mighty 18.6m (61ft) pole-hop over a canal.

Joe Darby cleared a full-length billiard table of 3.65m (12ft) in a single leap in 1892. Later someone told him the right way to move the balls was with a cue.

FOOD FOR THOUGHT

The 91.44m (100 yard) dash during which the winner never moved was won by **Peter Dowdeswell of Northamptonshire, Britain.** He took 21.7 seconds to eat that length of spaghetti – curled (fortunately) on the plate in front of him.

It's unlikely that Mrs Meltzer's boy chews his food properly when he eats. In 1974, Steve Meltzer of Brooklyn, New York wolfed down 96 sausages in 6 minutes. That's one every 4 seconds.

Fred Magel of Chicago, USA, a restaurant grader by trade, is also the world champion at dining out. He has eaten a grand total of 46,000 restaurant meals in 60 different countries. That's 42 uninterrupted years of eating out!

POOT POOT POOT POOT POOT POOT

SLURP!

It was probably in the Garden of Eden that man first discovered that the world was his oyster. So he ate it – and has been going strong ever since, happily gobbling just about anything that looks half-way interesting. Call it a healthy appetite, if you must, but then how do you account for these silly records?

When Dave Barnes goes to the seaside, all the clams in the area start to tremble and think about migration. In 1975, Dave wiped out 424, in just 8 minutes!

Karen Stevenson is proud to be called 'the queen of the has beans'. It was her great fondness for cold baked beans (there's no accounting for taste) that gave her this title. Using a cocktail stick, she daintly nibbled 2780 in 30 minutes in Merseyside, England in 1981.

DISH OF THE DAY

One of the biggest dishes on any menu is the stuffed roast camel sometimes served at Bedouin wedding feasts. 'Take one camel' the recipe starts. It continues with cooked eggs stuffed inside fish. The fish is stuffed into cooked chicken. The chicken goes inside a roast sheep, and the sheep into the camel. And how do you serve roast camel? With both hands!

WHAT'S THE DESERT DESSERT?

Ask a grocer, in Saudi Arabia, for a kilo of First Choice Black Perigord truffles and you'll be asked to shell out £40128.80 (At that price it's to be nibbled, not gulped.) This truffle, the most expensive food in the world, is usually sold in tiny 12.5g (0.44oz) tins at a price of £50.16 a time.

If all the chefs in all the world went out together and got drunk, they'd probably come up with a few of the recipes found on these pages. Only these are real recipes. Perhaps it just goes to show that when it comes to cooking, nothing succeeds like excess!

I'LL HAVE A PIZZA THAT!

Bakers are famous for making light cakes. But Chef Eichenauer of Atlantic City, USA went for the world's heaviest. It weighed 37.18 tonnes (81,982lb).

If you had been in Johannesburg, South Africa on 31st March 1984, you – and about 60,000 other people – could have had a slice of the same pizza. The largest ever baked, it was 26.4m (86ft 7in) wide and weighted 8465kg (7 tons).

What do you do with 20,000 bananas – apart from feel ill? Build the biggest banana split in the world, at 4.02km (2.5 miles) long! That's what they did at the Addison County Fair, in Vermont, USA, in 1984.

COME AND GET IT!

A cook in high gear is a wonder to behold. When Mark Pi of the China Gate Restaurant of Ohio set a noodle-making record, he churned out 2048 noodle strings in a phenomenal 34.5 seconds.

The Royal Navy is a cracking career, especially for cook John Bailey. On *HMS Brawdy*, in 1970, he knocked out a two-egg omelette every 7.5 seconds for 20 minutes, setting a world record of 240.

Squeamish readers look elsewhere. The question that follows might upset you. Question: What are you legally allowed to grill, beat, whip, cut, slice, sear. Answer: Food. Now read on.

Taking 11.5hrs to peel an apple may not be many people's idea of hard work. But when Kathy Wafler of New York set her mind to the job it was a narrow scrape. She ended up with a thin, unbroken strip of peel 52.51m (172ft 4in) long.

HAPPINESS IS AN UNSLICED CUKE!

The hand is faster than the eye at the championship level of cucumber slicing. Norman Johnson from Blackpool, England cut a 30.48cm (12in) cucumber into 244 slices in a blur of motion lasting 13.4 seconds (18 per sec)!

I THINK I'VE LOST MY APPLETITE!

When a 5-man team whittled their way through a 226.5kg (587lb 8oz) mountain of potatoes in just 45 minutes, their eyes were obviously bigger than their stomachs!

Peeling 22.67kg (50lb) of onions would be torture for most people. For Alfonso Salvo of Pennsylvania it was a piece of cake. There wasn't a dry eye in the house when he finished in 5mins 23secs.

HAVE A GOOD DAY

Most people start work after school and retire at 65. Not Shigechiyo Izumi. He began at a Japanese sugar mill in 1872 and retired as a farmer in 1970, 98 years later.

Good morse coders can acutally 'sing' the dots and dashes to each other. The fastest receiving speed is 72.2wpm. Sending speeds of 475 symbols per min have been measured.

Secretaries are often hired for speed – at the typewriter that is. The record on a manual machine is 176 words a minute. On electrics the score rises to 216 words.

Some people love their work – some hate it. Others sleep right through and wonder what all the fuss is about. But this is always true about work – it takes up a lot of precious time and energy that could otherwise be spent on really useful pastimes like flying kites or watching ants...

Long hours at the office are nothing compared to a hospital doctor's. Dr Paul Ashton's record 142 hour week left him just 3hr 43min a day for sleep!

HE'S MISSED A BIT!

THAT'S A CLOSE SHAVE!

Roy Ridley of Australia is on the ladder to success – he cleaned 3 standard office windows with water and a squeegee in 18.92 seconds. Most people prefer to let the rain do their dirty work for them.

Gerry Harley, the English barber with the accleration of a Ferrari, once shaved 987 men in one 60 minute sprint. Working with a safety razor, there were no bloody faces to earn him penalty points!

KEEP IT UP...

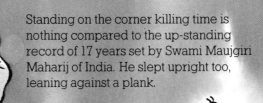

Standing on the corner killing time is nothing compared to the up-standing record of 17 years set by Swami Maujgiri Maharij of India. He slept upright too, leaning against a plank.

In an electrifying performance William Fuqua stayed motionless for 10hr 58min in front of crowd in a California shopping centre.

HE'S WARM AS TOAST!

Bad news for cannibals. It takes a lot of heat to cook human beings. In 1960, naked volunteers for the US Air Force endured dry air temperatures of up to 204.4°C (400°F), and 260°C (500°F) with heavy clothes on.

Most people can endure a certain amount of discomfort without ever bothering to complain. However, going out of your way to find new and horrible forms of discomfort to put up with is entirely another matter. It just goes to show that people will do almost anything to get their names up in lights.

Sitting up a tree sounds easy, until you try and do it for 431 consecutive days, like Timothy Roy in 1982–83. Maybe the trees of California have beds, showers and kitchens to make it all worthwhile!

Michael Moore must have thought he was a fish when he put on his scuba gear to spend 78hr 2min underwater in a swimming pool in Ireland. His biggest problem, it turned out, was keeping his skin from peeling off!

Bill White spent 141 days deep in the heart of Texas; 2m (6ft 6in) deep to be exact. He had himself buried in a coffin with only a thin tube for air, food and water!

KEEP ON KEEPING ON!

Cracking non-stop jokes for 42 hours needs a good source of inspiration. Fortunately Steve Emerald from, where else – Ireland – had plenty of gags from home!

Perhaps one of the reasons why Western Australia is so dry is because of Arron Marshall. He took a non-stop 336 hour shower, starting very dirty and ending up as clean as a whistle!

Risking flute and mouth disease, Joe Silmon of Hampshire, England set the longest record for continuous flute playing in 1977 – a breathless 48 hours.

Most people think that marathons have something to do with running. They are, in fact, really safety valves for those strange kinds of people who can't seem to get enough of a good thing. Long after parties have ended and the rest of us have gone home, marathon addicts keep on, and on, and on, and...

Eddie Leven certainly knew who he wanted – and kissed Delphine Crha for 17 days 9hrs to prove it; John McPherson couldn't make his mind up and kissed 4,444 different women in 8hrs! His lips are now in need of a retread.

RATHER YOU THAN ME BUDDY BOY!

The world record for non-stop talking was not set by an argument between a husband and wife team, but by a lecturer discussing the subject of Buddhist culture. Kapila Kumarasinghe, of Sri Lanka, talked for 159 hours – just 9 hours short of a solid week.

HOW REALLY, REALLY FASCINATING!

DON'T PULL A MUSCLE!

Belgian John Massis, known to his friends as 'Hercules', can never have suffered from a sweet tooth – his are the strongest in the world.

He has lifted 233kg (514lb) 15cm (6in) from the ground, and stopped a helicopter from taking off using only a tooth bit harness. Pity his dentist if he ever has to have a tooth extracted!

HE'S GOT HIMSELF INTO A TIGHT SPOT!

To build a house you've got to pick up bricks, and most sensible people do it with a hod – a Finn, Eric Stenman holds that record with 269kg (653lb) carried a distance of 5m (16ft), then up a 2m (6ft 6in) ramp.

Englishman Fred Burton chose to do it the difficult way, presumably to stretch himself to the limit. He picked up 24 bricks horizontally. They had a span of 1.5m (5ft) and weighed 51kg (112lb).

People will go to extraordinary lengths to prove just how strong they are — and not only by lifting weights either. that's far too boring in the eyes of those featured here. Somebody out there is probably trying to prove he's got the strongest big toe right now!

'Ullo Gary, got a new motor? Gary Windebank, from Hampshire, must have had more than one car in mind – he supported a total of 96 Michelin XZX 115×13's, a tiring 653kg (1440lb)!

Hotties are out – too dangerous – now it's meteorological balloons! Nick Mason, from Cheshire, blew up a huge 1000 gramme (35lb) monster to a 2.4m (7ft 10in) diameter in 70min 2secs . . . Pheeew!

MONEYBAGS

An Oklahoma rancher paid $300,000 in life insurance premiums in 1969. The following year he was murdered. His wife, Mrs Linda Mullendore, received the biggest ever payout on a single life – some $18 million in all.

I'LL NEVER INSURE A RANCHER AGAIN!

You know you're rich when the taxman gives you a warm grin. A banker, Nicholas Van Hoogstraten, was presented with a record tax demand of £5,371,220 in 1981.

LOOKS LIKE A NASTY ATTACK OF THE TAX MAN'S!

They say that money isn't everything. They also say that the only thing better than having money is having enough of it. For most of us, however, the problem is one of deciding just how much is enough. The lucky people on this page have none of these problems, they have more than enough...

With a personal fortune of over £200 million queen Wilhelmina, the former queen of the Netherlands was the world's richest woman.

Frederick Smith, chairman of Federal Express in the USA, earned $51,544,000 in 1982 ($25,000 an hour).

The Sultan of Brunei, who more or less owns the place lock, stock and oil barrel, has an annual income of $2,700 million making him the richest man in the world.

Where else but Hollywood! The child actor Jackie Coogan, co-star of Chaplin's 1920 film *The Kid*, was the youngest millionaire ever!

ON THE MOVE

Imitating a great moment in Bible history was not what Fritz Weber had in mind when he walked 300km (185 miles) down the River Main in Germany in 1983. He had the help of a pair of giant floating shoes!

The world champion at thumbing lifts is Ray Anderson. He hitched 468,219km (291,000 miles) – more than 11 times around the world – between 1969 and 1984.

In 1983, 13 members of the Aldington Prison Officers Club showed their clients a great idea by racing off in a paddled bathtub. They made 145.6km (90.5 miles) in 24 hours.

SEE YOU LATER DAVID!

WHEN I SAID GO FOR A PADDLE...

The record ordeal of trial by in-flight movie and pre-packed dinner was set by David Springbett of England, who flew 37,124km (23,068 miles) in 44hr 6min in 1980. This was the fastest time ever for a regularly scheduled trip around the world.

If it's true that travel broadens the mind, then these voyagers must have minds as wide as barn doors. One way or another, all of them have gone out of their way to make their journeys more difficult than necessary. It all goes to show that it's not so much where you go, as the way you travel, that counts.

Hot air doesn't only rise. It travels too. In 1972, a toy balloon released by Jane Dorst made a record 20 day flight from California to South Africa, a journey of 14,500km (9000 miles).

THIS'LL CUT HIM DOWN TO SIZE!

Where paddle steamers once ruled, paddle boats take their place. In 1979, Mick Sigrist and Brad Rud splashed a foot paddle boat 3582km (2226 miles) down the Mississippi to the Gulf of Mexico. The trip took them 103 days.

The longest journey ever undertaken on stilts was in 1980 by Joe Bowen. In 156 days he took the high road and stilt-walked 4804km (3008 miles) across America from Los Angeles to Bowen, Kentucky.

GREAT ESCAPES

The greatest life saver ever was lifeguard Leroy Columbo. The city of Galveston, Texas put up a plaque after his death to mark the 907 people he pulled out of the water in the years from 1917 to 1974.

CALL ME A JAIL BIRD!

WHAT ABOUT ME!

In 1979, a retired US Army colonel named Arthur Simons led a 14-man team into Gasre prison in Teheran to rescue 2 fellow Americans. In the confusion that ensued, other prisoners in the same jail followed his example and also made a break for it. 11,000 got out!

Given half a chance people will get themselves into terrible scrapes and yet, like kittens up trees, somehow still manage to escape. They have been rescued from the most incredible sorts of disasters: from rafts at sea, from the bottom of the ocean, from drowning, from jail, and even from unhappy marriages!

Second Steward Poon escaped on a raft, spending 133 days (4½ months) alone in the Atlantic, when his ship was torpedoed in 1943. He was well enough to walk ashore when he finally reached land!

OH GOOD! A TRAVEL SHOW!

HOLD ON! I'VE LEFT SOMETHING BEHIND!

Some idiot rammed the submersible *Nekton Beta*, with Richard Slater on board. He surfaced 58.58m (225ft) later, having escaped from the greatest depth with no equipment!

The latest ever escape from a disastrous marriage was by Harry Bidwell of England. He divorced his wife at the ripe old age of 101!

LITTLE AND LARGE

The hospital that admitted Jon Minnoch in 1978 had no scales that could take him, but his estimated weight was over 635kg (1400lb).

The lightest adult ever was a Mexican dwarf, Lucia Zarate, who weighed 2.125kg (4.7lb) at age 17. Thereafter she 'fattened up' to reach 5.9kg (13lb) at the age of 20 years.

HAPPY BIRTHDAY

The shortest fully grown person ever, was Pauline Musters. She was a midget who grew to only 59cm (23.2in) by age 19. A newborn baby is about 45.5cm (18–20in).

The greatest reliable age of any human being is 119 years for Shigechiyo Izumi of Japan. Born in 1865, he was still alive in 1985!

Whoever claimed that people are the same the world over, ignored the main thing that makes them really interesting – the incredible variety of human life to be found on our small planet. For example, just look at the extremes of human size and age, they sound like the stories fishermen tell of the ones that got away!

HE'S THE HEIGHT OF FASHION!

The only person to have been both a dwarf and a giant in his lifetime was Adam Rainer of Austria. At age 21 he stood 118cm (3ft 11in) high. In the next 11 years he grew to 215.9cm (7ft 1in), but became so weak he spent the rest of his life in bed.

BEFORE!

AFTER!

Robert Wadlow, the tallest man ever to live, was half an inch taller than his 5ft 11in father – at the age of 8! At age 22, the year of his death, he towered 2.72m (8ft 11in) and was still growing.

IF I REALLY TRY I MIGHT MAKE IT TOO!

ALL IN THE FAMILY

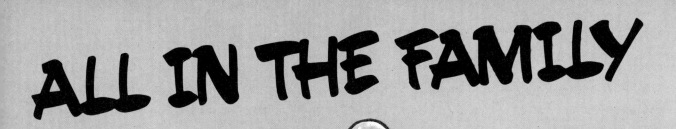

When Sheik Zayid ibn Said threw a small family wedding for his son Mohammed to Princess Salama; the party lasted 7 days and cost only £22 million. It was held in a purpose-built stadium for 20,000 guests.

The world's busiest (and probably most reliable) 'best man' ever is Wally Gant, a fishmonger from Wakefield, West Yorkshire. Himself a bachelor, he stood up to do his official duty for the 50th time in 33 years in 1964.

HOPE HE HASN'T LOST THE RING!

The longest delay between good intentions and doing right by your woman was 67 years, when Octavio Guillen and Adriane Martinez finally ended their engagement and married in 1969. Both were 82 at the time.

If you think that two children, two parents, a pet and a dozen houseplants is the normal size of a normal family, then prepare yourself for a shock. Families come in all shapes and sizes. They also have a wonderful knack of making people behave in the strangest ways imaginable...

The greatest number of children born to one mother is 69. The first wife of a Russian peasant from Shuya, Feodor Vassilyev (1707–82), put even rabbits to shame by giving birth to 4 sets of quads, 7 sets of triplets and 16 twins.

On Susan Kistler's 18th birthday her mum was 75, and a bit. So what? you might say – just that it made her 57 when Susan was born, and the oldest mum ever to give birth!

NAME THAT TUNE!

The longest stint of solo singing was a marathon 180hr·(7½ days) by Robert Sim, at the Waterfront Hotel in England.

The shortest opera ever performed is *The Deliverance of Theseus* which lasts a merciful 7min 27sec. By comparison, the longest *The Heretics* rackets on for 8½hr.

The biggest one-man band ever recorded was conducted and manned by Rory Blackwell. He played 4 melody and 20 percussion instruments simultaneously in TV South West Studios, Devon, UK.

HAVE YOU GOT THE RIGHT TIME?

Human beings love making noise. Whether singing in the shower, or singing in the rain, all of them thrill to the sound of music — more or less. But it takes a musician, using every trick in the book, to really stir up excitement. And that's what the best musicians spent their time doing — stirring it up!

MUST BE A VERY FAST PIECE OF MUSIC!

The highest price ever to be paid for a piano was $390,000 for a 100 year old Steinway grand. It was bought in 1980 at an auction in New York City by an over-excited bidder who could't even play the thing!

♫ ROLL OVER BEETHOVEN! ♫

The largest orchestra ever to be heard had 20,100 players. It was made up of bands from all over Norway, and assembled once to play in an Oslo stadium in 1964.

COME DANCING...

The fastest tap dancer on record, Roy Castle, hit 1440 taps per minute (24 per second) in front of TV cameras on BBC *Record Breakers* programme in 1973.

After a performance of Swan Lake in Vienna, Dame Margot Fonteyn and Rudolf Nureyev received 89 curtain calls, the most ever for a ballet.

HE'S DEAD ON HIS FEET!

The most gruelling dance marathon ever staged lasted 5148hr 28min from 1930 to 1931. It was won by Mike Ritof and Edith Boudreaux of Chicago, USA. The prize was $2000 (or 39 cents and hour)!

Dancing is the most exciting pastime in the world, and the reason is quite simple. The hotter the music, the more worked-up people become – the more excited they get, the more they try to outdo everyone else on the dance floor. Best of all – everyone has a good time. What could be more harmless?

The longest ever conga snake was one that included 8659 people, all members of the **Camping and Caravaning Club of Great Britain.**

All the stage is awhirl during the 32 spins in *Swan Lake*, the greatest number of continuous turns called for in any classical ballet.

Limbo dancer, **Marlene Raymond,** passed under a flaming limbo bar that was 15.5cm (6⅛in) high, with only her feet touching the floor!

DOES CRIME PAY?

The greatest art robbery of all time took place in Ireland in 1974. Four men and a woman stole 19 paintings, worth about £8,000,000, from the home of Sir Alfred Beit.

The biggest sum ever extorted by hijackers was $6,000,000 when a Japan Airlines DC-8 was grabbed at Dacca Airport, Bangladesh in 1977 with 38 hostages on board.

The biggest killer ever was Behram, an Indian Thugee cult member. He strangled 931 victims to death with a yellow and white strip of cloth in the years between 1790 and 1840!

It is often claimed that crime doesn't pay. Perhaps that's the reason why Al Capone, the American gangster, called himself a 'secondhand furniture dealer' on his business card. He was looking for a respectable business that could help to explain how he managed to earn over $100 million a year!

Between 1964 and 1973, some 64,000 fake insurance policies were cooked up on the Equity Funding Corporation computer. They were valued at about $2 billion.

The biggest crime operation in the world is the Mafia. With about 5000 people in 25 'families', it earns some $200 billion a year.

The youngest person ever kidnapped was Carolyn Wharton. She was whisked from her Texas hospital crib, 29 minutes after being born, by a woman dressed as a nurse!

BIZZARE PURSUITS

The record for lying on a bed of sharp 15.2cm (6in) nails is 273hr (no tossing and turning allowed), set by Alan Andrew of Wales in 1983. For the last 34hr he had company. His fiancee, Katherine Weston, lay beside him on a similar bed. It was a prickly start to a life of married bliss!

The greatest number of lions ever to be mastered by a single lion-tamer, and then fed in the same cage, is 40. Captain Alfred Schneider was the brave man who tried this stunt in 1925.

People take up the strangest pastimes to keep themselves amused. They devote immense effort to learning odd bits of information, or to performing bizarre stunts. Often as not, the dangers involved are very real and the rewards are simply the pleasure of doing it. So why do they bother in the first place?

A pyramid of 6 cheerleaders at the University of California, sprayed with a chemical attractant, made a 'beard' of bees in 1983 that smothered them from head to toe.

WHERE'S THAT PIE?

Most people find it hard to recall phone numbers. Rajan Srinivasen of India, however, memorised 'pi' to 31,811 numbers. It took him 3hr 49min to recite them all!

A team of 9 employees of an Edinburgh bedding centre pushed a hospital bed 5204km (3233 miles 1150 yards) in 1979 to set a record for the longest bed roll ever.

HE'S WET THE BED!

HAVING A SMASHING TIME!

WHAT A WAY TO EARN A LIVING!

Some people just hate music – rather than tickle the ivories they prefer to take a sledge-hammer to them. The Tinwald Rugby Football Club from New Zealand are the boys when it comes to making not-so-sweet music with an old joanna – they demolished an entire upright, putting the bits through a 22cm (8½in) circle, in 1min 37secs! Three young men from Nottingham didn't have any sledgehammers, so they used their bare hands and feet to do the job in 2min 35secs!

When a doctor told M. Mangetout (Michel Lotito) of France to put some more iron in his diet little did he know that he would go off and eat 7 bicycles and TV sets, a supermarket trolley and a lo-cal Cessna light aircraft! He's now got a magnetic personality.

SUCH A PLANE DIET!

STAINLESS STEEL TOOTHPICKS

LO-CAL

Most of what we know about the past comes from what was left behind – if the characters here are anything to go by future generations of historians are going to have a very hard time piecing together what we were up to!

Evel Knievel seems to get into the record books more for his failures than successes as a stunt man – in fact his failure to jump the 485m (1591ft) wide, 180m (590ft) deep Snake River Canyon earned him $6 million! By the end of his '85 season Evel had suffered 433 bone fractures – and there are only 206 bones in the human body!

Luckily Dick Sheppard's business is wrecking cars, otherwise his insurance bill would be enormous – he has smashed up 1,839 vehicles in his stunt career!

SPARES

5,000 ft

TWO'S COMPANY

Jumbo jets are built to carry up to 500 people. In 1974 they packed 306 adults, 328 kids and 40 babies (total 674) into one on a flight from cyclone-devastated Darwin to Sydney.

AND THEY SAY I'M OVERWEIGHT!

YOU JUST NEED SMALL FRIENDS

The most passengers ever to squeeze on to a bicycle is 16, when members of Tokyo cycle club climbed on to one and rode for 50m (164ft).

The most people ever to cram themselves on to a pillar box is 32. All were students of Wentworth College, York, England. None were delivered!

Rush hour is a silly human invention, designed to get as many people as possible, into the smallest vehicle that can be found. Hopefully, but not always, one that will move. If there isn't a rush hour handy, some people will set out with great determination to make one of their own.

By really putting their backs into it, 14 members of the Phi Gamma Delta Club, Seattle, USA, leap-frogged a total of 108,463 times in 114hrs – 968.8km (602 miles)!

The biggest game of musical chairs on record started with 4514 players and ended with Scott Ritter faced the music sitting on the last chair.

POESN'T ANYONE NEED A CHAIR?

The largest number of people ever to be seated as if on a chair, but without using chairs, were the 10,323 employees of the Nissan Motor Company of Japan in 1982. Each person was squeezed between two others to make a huge unsupported circle.

WHAT HAPPENS WHEN SOME ONE GETS UP?

EXERCISE YOUR RIGHTS

WE HAVE LIFT-OFF!

Weighted clubs can be used to exercise the arms and chest. Albert Rayner got into the swing of things, and set a 60min record in 1981, whirling a club 17,512 times.

The largest male chest record is held by fatman Robert Hughes, who weighed 485kg (1069lb). He had a massive 264cm (104in) chest.

The most people ever to skip together was a line of 160 Japanese high school students. They leaped a single 50m rope more than 12 times.

If exercise is good for you, and even more exercise is better, then the most exercise you can do should be best of all. Not true — all it will do is win you some of the records described below — but you'll be far too tired to enjoy the fame, and probably be too muscle-bound to get through your door...

YOU CAN DO IT! HUP–ONE–TWO! HUP–ONE–TWO!

24.000

The greatest number of two-handed push-ups performed non-stop is 24,300 by Jeffrey Warwich at the YMCA, Buffalo, NY, USA.

The record for walking on hands is 1400km (871 miles) from Vienna to Paris set by Johann Hurlinger is 1900; at an averge speed of 2.54km/h (1.58mph).

PARIS

Starting from a fully-extended 'dead hang' position on two arms, the most chin-ups ever made were 170 by Lee Yong of Seoul, Korea.

LITTLE WONDERS!

The greatest success at splitting hairs was by a man with a barber's sure touch. Alfred West split a human hair by hand into 18 parts!

Ten green bottles is nothing compared to the collection of 26,794 different miniature bottles assembled by David Maund, as of April 1985.

The smallest coin ever to have been minted is the Nepalese silver ¼ Jawa of 1740 which weighed .002 grams. It takes a mound of 493,920 to weigh one kilogram.

The world's smallest rideable bike is no bigger than a shoe. It has wheels only 3.5cm (1.37in) high.

There are records for smallness as well as for bigness, and the biggest records for the smallest things are incredibly tiny indeed – Is that clear? All of the following are examples of very small things that belong to, are used by, or are done by people just like you. No tricks and no machines were used…

Most people put stamps on letters, not Frank Watts – he puts letters on stamps. With no mechanical aid he can write the Lord's Prayer 34 times on the back of a standard UK stamp – 21.3×18.03mm (0.84×0.71in)!

The tiniest bone of the human body is the stirrup bone of the middle ear. It is from 2.6 to 3.4mm (0.1–0.17in) long and weighs around five hundreths of a gram.

The record of threading the 1.6mm (¹⁄₁₆in) eye of a number 13 needle – 3795 times in 2hr – was set by Brenda Robinson in 1971.

FOOLS RUSH IN ...

DON'T LOOK DOWN!

The longest T-bone dive off a ramp to land on a 'cushion' of parked cars, was 59.86m (196ft 5in) by Jean Pierre Vignan in a Ford Capri 2.6!

LOOKS MY LIKE LUNCH!

The highest tightrope cable ever, was across a gorge at the top of the Zugspitz mountain. Steve McPeak walked 181 steps across it with a drop of 960m (3150ft) below him.

The most intrepid stowaway ever was Socarras Ramirez of Cuba who rode 8hr in a DC-8 wheel well and survived −22°C (−8°F) temperatures at a height of 9145m (30,000ft).

Most people take life's difficulties in their stride. But it's the impossible, to which they stampede in order to have a go. Any number of people (other than Hollywood stuntmen) risk life and limb, simply trying out things which are more dangerous than they have tried before...

THAT COULD STUNT YOUR GROWTH!

Grant Page, a film stuntman, slid 91.4m (300ft) down a wire (with another person over the shoulder) from a starting height of 53.3m (175ft)!

In 1977, an unknown human fly, disguised by a mask, rode atop a DC-8 jet at speeds up to 480km/h (240mph). It would have been easier if he'd paid his fare!

UNDER THE BIG TOP

I KNOW WHAT THEY'RE THINKING!

The highest aerial act on a trapeze was performed by Celeste Starr underneath a cable car. The car, the Teleferico Merida, was 4763m (15,629ft) up a Venezuelan mountain at the time.

Charlie Revel, the oldest performing clown in the business, started at the age of 3 in 1899 and continued for 82 years until 1981.

A juggling record that may one day be broken by a clever seal was set by Gran Picaso of Spain in 1971. He kept 5 balls in the air at once – using only his mouth.

Everybody loves the excitement of a circus, and acts that range from clowns and small dogs, lion tamers, sword swallowers and daring high wire stunts. Today, the biggest travelling circus in the world is Circus Vargas of the USA. It can pack 5000 people under it's Big Top tent!

Tahar Davis, of the Hassani Troupe, supported a total weight of 771kg (1700lb) in the shape of the world's biggest inverted human pyramid – it rose three storeys above him!

Henri Rochetain of France spent 185 days on a 120m (394ft) tightrope in 1973. He even managed to sleep on the wire without falling off!

With a muzzle velocity of 86.9km/h (54mph), Emanuel Zacchini set the human cannonball record in 1940. He blasted 53.3m (175ft) across Madison Square Gardens, New York.

I PREFER TO DO IT... ...BLIND!

RIDICULOUS RECORDS!

WON'T SHE BE SURPRISED!

The biggest bubblegum bubble blown by Susan Montgomery of California in 1979 was 48.9cm (19¼in); almost twice the size of her head!

Randy Ober of Arkansas, USA splattered the world record when he spat a wad of tabacco 15.5m (47ft 7in) in 1982.

PHEW!! LICK THAT!

Frankie Howerd, the British comedian, may yet become known as old rubber tongue. He tore 72 stamps from a full sheet and individually licked and stuck them down on to envelopes all within a 4 minute time limit in 1984.

Records of achievement also exist for some of the very silly activities that distinguish human beings from, for instance, the more intelligent members of the animal world. Though simple enough to try out at home, the skill needed to match these feats takes years of dedicated practice...

COUGH! WHAT A DRAG!

David Donoghue scrambled a helicopter to 198m (650ft) and from there dropped a fresh egg on to a Tokyo Golf Course without it breaking!

I LIKE MINE SUNNYSIDE UP, PLEASE!

From a single drag on a cigarette, Jan Van Deurs Formann of Switzerland blew 355 individual smoke rings in 1979, the largest number ever achieved.

Roger Bourban, the racing waiter, ran the London marathon in 2hr 47min in full uniform holding an open bottle on a tray.

RAISING THE ROOF...

Beating the Swiss at their own game, Errol Bird of Northern Ireland yodelled non-stop for 26hr, between 27–28th September, 1984!

THIS WOULD MAKE A NICE NEST!

Motor-mouth John Moschitta of the USA once talked at a rate of 552 words per minute (10 a second) – and could still be understood!

Bucking the odds, girls normally have higher voices than boys, Neil Stephenson hit the loudest human voice yet recorded – 123.3dB!

Robert 'Sing It Again' Sim kept himself awake, fed and watered while singing solo for a record 180hr (7½ days) in 1983.

When is a racket not a racket? When it's a sound made by people instead of animals or machines. That's why we use polite words like talking, singing, whistling, shouting and yodelling to describe the terrible noise with which we fill the world – and when it comes to terrible noises, these are the champions.

Roy Lomas of England has the loudest known human whistle. When recorded by the BBC in 1983 it registered an ear-piercing 122.5 decibels at 2.5m (8ft).

THAT'LL TEACH HIM TO BELLOW!

Actors who love applause flocked to hear Ashrita Furman set a non-stop clapping record of 50hr 17min in New York in 1981.

The loudest repeat winner of the national town criers' contest is Ben Johnson of Cornwall, England who bellowed the news to win 11 times between 1939 and 1973.

SILLIER AND SILLIER

Using a blanket, 2 sheets, 1 pillow, 1 undersheet, 1 counterpane and hospital corners, Catheryn Marsden and Judith Strange set a British bed making record of 24 seconds.

IT'S ONE WAY OF GETTING UP!

NOT TODAY, THANKS!

In 1983, Brian Newton stunned tired bag-toting shoppers, by carrying a 50.8kg (1cwt) bag of coal for 51.5km (32 miles) in 10hr 18min.

For 13 days 43 min, life was a dizzy whirl of non-stop travel for Dana Dover, Chris Lyons and Gary Mandau. Sadly, they visited no exotic places for their marathon trip was on a merry-go-round!

The reason there is no competition for the silliest record in the world, is because there's no way of measuring silliness. For instance, if we used a unit like the 'centiclown', different feats could be rated against each other. Anyhow, here are five, all of which score at least 90 centiclowns or more.

Real men don't nibble grapes – they catch them as they fly by. In 1982, Paul Tavilla caught a grape in his mouth hurled 97.9m from (321ft 5in) from a 31-storey building!

FACT IS, HE CAN'T STAND LIFTS!

150th FLOOR

Dale Neil pounded up and down flights of stairs in the Peachtree Plaza Hotel in Atlanta, Georgia to set a record for running a vertical miles in 2hr 1min 25 seconds.

ALL IN THE GAME

THINK I'LL STICK TO POLO!

The highest wave ever to have been surfed was a tidal wave (or tsunami) some 15.24m (50ft) tall. It hit Minole, Hawaii in 1868 where it was ridden by a Hawaiian named Holua, desperate to save himself from being drowned, had the wave crashed over him.

Elephant polo was first played in Jaipur, India in 1976. Each beast carried 3 riders; one steering at the head, a club-wielding player, and a standing rider at the rump!

The earliest records of sport are of wrestling, dating from around 2750-2600 BC. In Egypt, murals of 2050 BC show girls playing ball games. Since then, sports have developed to include almost every imaginable form of ball game, and also death-defying activities from rock-climbing to sky-diving...

A. J. Lewis must have been truly myopic – he putted 156 times on one green and never got the ball in. Maybe there was a mole in the hole!

The tallest basketball player of all time was Suleiman Ali Nashnush. He stood 2.4m (8ft) tall and played with no great distinction on the Libyan national team of 1962!

The fastest ball game in the world is said to be pelota (or Jai Alai) where the ball travels at speeds of up to 302km/h (188mph).

TWO MORE GREAT TOUCAN TITLES FOR YOU TO COLLECT... NOW!

Bullet Trains and Underwater Tricycles

Bullet Trains and Underwater Tricycles brings you the amazing mechanical records from the **Guinness Book of Records**, collected here in one uproarious volume.

Mechanical developments since the wheel have progressed to the 50' long 10 wheel ultra limo – with its own 12' swimming pool in the boot! But in between there have been some noteworthy and quite extraordinary inventions – the 38 mph sailboard, the Rocket Flame car cruising at 622 mph and of course the heavies lead by the Terex Titan dumper weighing in at 539 tons. Visualise the subway escalator 195 long with 729 steps and the penknife with 1,822 blades.

Bomber Bats and Flying Frogs

Bomber Bats and Flying Frogs concentrates on astonishing lives within the animal kingdom – hundreds of animal facts everybody will want at their fingertips.

You didn't know that a baby kangaroo is only 1 inch long at birth! That termite colonies are centrally heated! That Ribbon worms eat themselves! That lobsters migrate in single file – holding claws – just a taste (if you'll excuse the expression). **Bomber Bats and Flying Frogs** assembles the unique facts from the animal kingdom that will endlessly fascinate any junior animalologist.